## Lut
### PBUH

عليه السلام

**FROM PROPHETS STORIES IN THE QUR'AN**

Prepared by:
Dr. Mohamed El Mouelhi

إعداد: د. محمد المويلحي

To My Grandchildren,
My Inspiration.
- Giddo M.

Text Copyright © 2022 by Mohamed El Mouelhi.
Artwork Copyright © 2022 by Hossam El Mouelhi and Donia Farouk.

All Rights Reserved. No part of this book may be reproduced, transmitted, or stored in an information retrieval system in any form or by any means, graphic, electronic, or mechanical, including photocopying, taping, and recording, without prior written permission from the publisher.

جميع الحقوق محفوظة.

ISBN 978-1-7357701-9-2

First edition 2022

Published by Honey Elm Books LLC
www.HoneyElmBooks.com

# Lut (Lot) PBUH

## لوط عليه السلام

**Editing: Noha Elmouelhi**

**Artistic Preparation: Hossam El Mouelhi - Donia Farouk**

تحرير: نهى المويلحي
الإعداد الفني: حسام المويلحي – دنيا فاروق

Prophet Lut PBUH
was the nephew of Prophet Ibrahim.
Lut believed in his uncle Ibrahim's call
to worship only Allah and migrated
with him to Jordan.
Lut lived near his uncle in a village near the Jordan River
valley in an area with fertile soil.

كان النبي لوط ابن شقيق النبي إبراهيم عليهما السلام، وقد آمن برسالته لعبادة الله وحده. وعاش لوط بعد أن هاجر مع إبراهيم في قرية بالقرب من وادي نهر الأردن في منطقة ذات تربة خصبة.

The people of Lut deviated from the main purpose of having humans on earth which is to inhabit it and to reproduce through the natural relationship between male and female for all creatures, whether human, animal or plant.

وكان قوم لوط ابتعدوا عن الغرض الأساسى لوجود الإنسان على الأرض وهو عمارتها والتكاثر فيها، والذي يتم عن طريق العلاقة الطبيعية بين الذكر والأنثى لكل المخلوقات سواء بشر أو حيوان أو نبات.

The people of Lut ignored the natural course of humanity and instead turned to homosexuality - an act never before seen in humanity.

They also engaged in other sins, such as robbing travelers.

ولكن قوم لوط اتجهوا الى الفاحشة التي لم يسبقهم إليها أحد من العالمين، ألا وهي إقامة علاقات بين الرجال بعضهم البعض، كما قاموا بقطع طريق المارة وسلب ممتلكاتهم وعمل الفاحشة معهم.

"And (remember) Lut, when he said to his people:'You commit an indecency wherein none has preceded you in the worlds. (28) Verily, you practice sodomy with men, and rob the travelers! And practice evil wicked deeds in your meetings …'" (Al-Ankaboot:28 - 29)

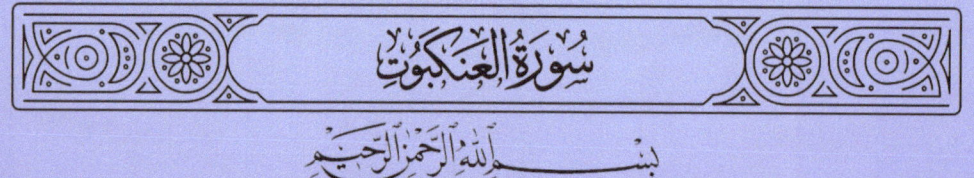

وَلُوطًا إِذْ قَالَ لِقَوْمِهِ إِنَّكُمْ لَتَأْتُونَ ٱلْفَٰحِشَةَ مَا سَبَقَكُم بِهَا مِنْ أَحَدٍ مِّنَ ٱلْعَٰلَمِينَ ۝ أَئِنَّكُمْ لَتَأْتُونَ ٱلرِّجَالَ وَتَقْطَعُونَ ٱلسَّبِيلَ وَتَأْتُونَ فِى نَادِيكُمُ ٱلْمُنكَرَ ۖ ... ۝

Allah sent Lut as His prophet
to call on them to return to the
ways of Allah, to abstain from doing evil sins,
and to repent to Allah.
But the people of Lut didn't listen and continued
their sinful acts. Lut warned them of Allah's torment
and punishment. They mocked him and threatened him
that if he continued to preach to them,
they would run him out of their village.

أرسل الله لوطاً لدعوة قومه الى طاعة الله وترك الفاحشة والتوبة منها، ولكن قوم لوط لم يستمعوا لدعوته وأستمروا فى عمل المنكر والفاحشة، فحذرهم لوط من عذاب الله وإنتقامه منهم، فاستهزؤا به وهددوه إن إستمر فى دعوته فإنهم سيطردونه من قريتهم.

"There was no other answer given by his people except that they said: `Drive out the family of Lut from your city. Verily, these are men who want to be clean and pure!' "
(Al-Naml:56)

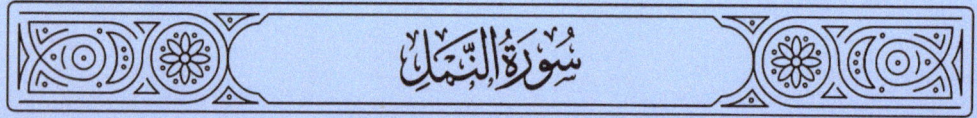

بِسْمِ ٱللَّهِ ٱلرَّحْمَٰنِ ٱلرَّحِيمِ

فَمَا كَانَ جَوَابَ قَوْمِهِ إِلَّآ أَن قَالُوٓاْ أَخْرِجُوٓاْ ءَالَ لُوطٍ مِّن قَرْيَتِكُمْ ۖ إِنَّهُمْ أُنَاسٌ يَتَطَهَّرُونَ ۝

Lut's people insisted on defying him and continued their sinful deeds, and Lut repeatedly warned them of Allah's punishment.
They mocked him and asked him to inflict upon them the punishment that he promised.
Lut asked Allah to save him and his family from this village and the indecent acts of its people.

وتمادى قوم لوط فى تكذيبه وأستمروا فى أعمالهم القبيحة، وحذرهم لوط مراراً من عذاب الله، فاستهزؤا به وطلبوا منه أن ينزل عليهم العذاب الذى وعدهم به، ودعا لوط الله أن ينجيه هو وأهله من هذه القرية ومن عمل قومها الفاحش.

Allah accepted Lut's prayer
and sent His angels to Lut's village and his people.

وإستجاب الله لدعاء لوط، فأرسل ملائكته الى القرية التى يقيم بها لوط وأهله.

When the angels arrived
to Lut's village in the form of men,
he didn't recognize them. He invited them
to his home as his guests to protect them from
the evil of his people.
Lut's wife secretly told the townspeople about the strange
guests. So they went to Lut looking for his guests.
Lut got angry and tried to prevent them from harming his
guests, but they insisted on encroaching on Lut's guests.

وعندما ذهب الملائكة الى قرية لوط فى هيئة رجال فلم يعرفهم لوط، ولكنه أستضافهم عنده لحمايتهم من شر قومه. وعرف قومه بضيوفه عندما أبلغتهم زوجة لوط بالضيوف الغرباء، فذهبوا إليه رغبة فى هؤلاء الضيوف. وغضب لوط وحاول منعهم من إيذاء ضيوفه ولكنهم أصروا على التعدى عليهم.

"And his people came rushing towards him, and since aforetime they used to commit crimes indecencies... " (Hud:78)

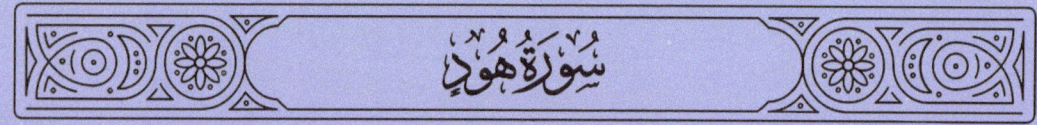

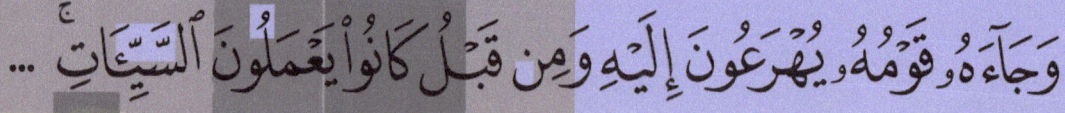

Lut was very upset and asked Allah to punish his people for their indecent acts.

Then the guests told Lut that they were angels sent by Allah to inflict punishment on his people in the morning and they would save him and his family except his wife.

وإزداد غضب لوط ودعا ربه أن يعاقب قومه لسوء أعمالهم، وعندها أخبر الضيوف لوطاً أنهم ملائكة مرسلين من الله لإنزال العذاب بقومه في الصباح وأنهم سينجُوه هو وأهله إلا إمرأته.

"He said: 'I am, indeed, of those who hate your conduct.(168) My Lord! Save me and my family from what they do.' "(169)
(Al-Shuara)

قَالَ إِنِّى لِعَمَلِكُم مِّنَ ٱلْقَالِينَ ۝ رَبِّ نَجِّنِى وَأَهْلِى مِمَّا يَعْمَلُونَ ۝

That night,
Lut and the believers left town.
In the morning, Allah sent down His torment
on the disbelieving people of Lut by raining
stones on them.
Their city was completely destroyed and the wrongdoers
of the people of Lut vanished. The remains of the villages
and homes of the people of Lut became a warning
to humanity throughout the ages and permanent evidence of
Allah's ability to punish the corrupters on earth.

وغادر لوط القرية في هذه الليلة والمؤمنون معه.
وفي الصباح أنزل الله عذابه بقوم لوط بأن أمطرهم بحجارة مصوبة عليهم
فدمرت مدينتهم تماماً وأهلكت الظالمين من قوم لوط، وأصبحت بقايا
قرى قوم لوط وبيوتهم تحذيراً للبشرية على مر العصور، ودليلاً
قائما على قدرة الله على معاقبة المفسدين
في الأرض.

"So when Our Commandment came, We turned (the towns of Sodom) upside down, and rained on them stones of baked clay, in a well-arranged manner one after another" (Hud:82)

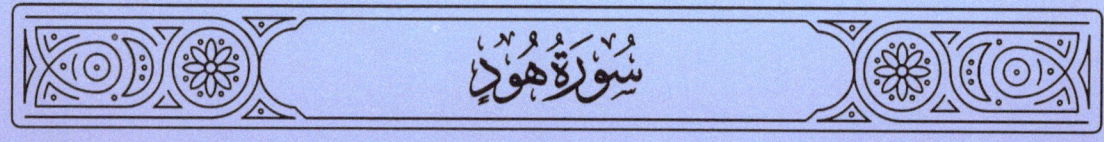

فَلَمَّا جَآءَ أَمْرُنَا جَعَلْنَا عَٰلِيَهَا سَافِلَهَا وَأَمْطَرْنَا عَلَيْهَا حِجَارَةً مِّن سِجِّيلٍ مَّنضُودٍ ﴿٨٢﴾

Lut and his people
are mentioned in the Qur'an 27 times
as a reminder for us to learn from their sins
and always remember the way of Allah.
The religion of Allah is the One, True way
and we must hold fast to it, even when
our society around us is changing.

ذُكر لوط عليه السلام وقومه 27 مرة فى القرآن الكريم، وهذا للتنبيه على سوء الفاحشة وعقاب الله الشديد لمرتكبيها.
ودين الله هو الحق والهادى الى الطريق المستقيم، فيجب علينا التمسك به حتى لو تغير المجتمع من حولنا.

# Watch a special reading of Lut PBUH by the author!

Scan this QR code to access the video.

www.ingramcontent.com/pod-product-compliance
Lightning Source LLC
Chambersburg PA
CBHW040023130526
44590CB00036B/80